MIGUEL HIDALGO Y COSTILLA

FATHER OF MEXICAN INDEPENDENCE

FRANK DE VARONA

Hispanic Heritage
The Millbrook Press
Brookfield, Connecticut

Facing page: In this mural by Mexican artist José Clemente Orozco, Father Hidalgo rises up in fiery revolt against Spain.

Cover photograph courtesy of Instituto Latinoamericano de La Comunicación Educativa

Photographs courtesy of Schalkwijk/Art Resource, New York: p. 3; Rakoczy/Art Resource, New York: p. 4; Instituto Latinoamericano de La Comunicación Educativa: pp. 6, 19, 27; Bettmann: p. 11; Culver Pictures: pp. 13, 16, 23; Laurie Platt Winfrey, Inc.: pp. 14, 15, 20, 21, 28; Lutteroth-Uribe/AMI/Art Resource, New York: p. 24; Presidencia de la Republica/AMI/Art Resource, New York: p. 29.

Map by Joe LeMonnier

Library of Congress Cataloging-in-Publication Data

de Varona, Frank.
Miguel Hidalgo y Costilla : father of Mexican independence / by Frank de Varona.
p.   cm.—(Hispanic heritage)
Includes bibliographical references and index.
Summary: Relates the life story of the Catholic priest who became an activist in working to free Mexico from Spanish rule.
ISBN 1-56294-370-7 (lib. bdg.) ISBN 1-56394-863-6 (pbk.)
1. Hidalgo y Costilla, Miguel, 1753–1811—Juvenile literature.
2. Mexico—History—Wars of Independence, 1810–1821—Juvenile literature.   3. Revolutionaries—Mexico—Biography—Juvenile literature.   4. Catholic Church—Mexico—Clergy—Biography—Juvenile literature.   [1. Hidalgo y Costilla, Miguel, 1753–1811.
2. Revolutionaries.   3. Clergy.   4. Mexico—History—Wars of Independence, 1810–182.]   I. Title.   II. Series.
F1232.H57D4   1993
972'.03'092—dc20   [B]   92-36562   CIP   AC

Published by The Millbrook Press
2 Old New Milford Road
Brookfield, Connecticut 06804

MIGUEL
HIDALGO Y COSTILLA

In this mural by Mexican artist Diego Rivera, Father Hidalgo stands at the center of important figures in Mexican history. The banner at the top reads: Land and Liberty.

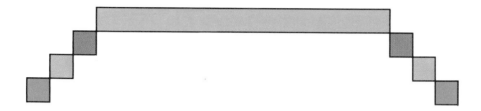

The Spanish soldier told the Mexican priest Miguel Hidalgo y Costilla that tomorrow Hidalgo would be shot. The priest was expecting this news. He had spent the last seventy-one days in jail and had seen many of his followers killed. All died for the same reason: They had fought behind Hidalgo to try to free Mexico from Spain's rule.

Because Hidalgo was a Catholic priest as well as the leader of the revolt against Spain—called the Mexican War of Independence—the decision to kill him took a long time. But on July 29, 1811, a court under the control of the Spanish government sentenced Hidalgo to die before a firing squad the following morning.

On the night before his execution, Hidalgo prayed and read the Bible. He wrote two poems on the walls of his prison cell. They were about the kindness of the two guards assigned to him.

At dawn on July 30, Father Hidalgo awoke. He was served his last breakfast. He noticed that he had been given less milk than usual. He joked to one guard that, just because he was going to die that day, he should not be given less milk.

At seven o'clock that morning, Hidalgo was led before a firing squad of twelve soldiers. To show his forgiveness to them, he gave them some pieces of candy. Seated in front of the squad with his eyes blindfolded, he placed one hand over his heart and said: "The right hand which I place on my chest, my sons, will be a certain target for your aims." Then, as he waited for the sentence to be carried out, he prayed aloud: "Have mercy upon me, O Lord!"

A fanciful painting of Father Hidalgo before the firing squad. In truth, he sat and was blindfolded.

The soldiers fired. Some were trembling and missed the target. But others did not miss. Hidalgo's body slumped forward in the chair. Two tears trickled down his cheeks. Two additional shots ended his life.

Spanish soldiers then cut off Hidalgo's head and placed it with the heads of his closest followers in iron cages. They hung these cages at the four corners of a fort called the Alhóndiga de Granaditas. Hidalgo and his followers had captured this fort before their struggle to free Mexico from Spain failed.

The Spanish government thought that the public showing of the heads would strike fear in others who wanted liberty. The Spaniards were mistaken. In ten years Mexico would be free from Spain. Miguel Hidalgo y Costilla would go down in history as the "Father of Mexican Independence."

CHILDHOOD · Hidalgo was born on May 8, 1753, on the Hacienda San Diego Corralejo, in the town of Pénjamo, Mexico. *"Hacienda"* is a Spanish word meaning a large farm. His parents were Cristóbal Hidalgo y Costilla and Ana María Gallega y Villaseñor.

His father's ancestors had come to Mexico from Spain many generations before. Mexico had been Spain's colony—property ruled by the European country across the sea—since the 1500s. In fact, during Spanish rule the colony was known as New Spain, not as Mexico.

ALASKA

NEW SPAIN
IN 1810

OREGON
COUNTRY

BRITISH
NORTH
AMERICA

UNITED STATES

ATLANTIC
OCEAN

VICEROYALTY
OF
NEW SPAIN

SPANISH
FLORIDA

Mexico City

CUBA

SANTO DOMINGO

PUERTO RICO

Caribbean Sea

The Viceroyalty of New Spain stretched from
Central America through Mexico and far into
North America.

THE PEOPLE
OF NEW SPAIN

By 1810, New Spain included Mexico, Central America, and what are now Texas, New Mexico, Arizona, California, Nevada, and parts of Utah, Wyoming, and Colorado. Almost six million people lived in New Spain. Among them were:

▪ *15,000 people born in Spain.* These people, called *gachupines*, had the best jobs in the colony. They held the most important positions in the government, the army, and the Church. They also owned much of the land.

▪ *600,000 Creoles.* Like Miguel's father's ancestors, these people's ancestors originally came from Spain. Mexican Creoles did not like the fact that they came second in importance after the Spaniards. They could not get the best-paying jobs and felt mistreated in their own country.

▪ *1.5 million mestizos.* These people were the children or descendants of intermarriages between Native Americans and Spaniards or Creoles. Mestizos held low-level jobs on the haciendas and in the army.

▪ *3.5 million Native Americans.* Although these people were the territory's original inhabitants, they could not own land and lived in poverty. Most worked in the fields for up to sixteen hours a day.

▪ *10,000 black slaves from Africa.* These people had no freedoms or rights.

Miguel's mother was also born in New Spain. She was the descendant of a man by the name of Juan de Villaseñor. Villaseñor founded the important Mexican city of Valladolid, known today as Morelia. This distinguished background made Miguel's family one of the most important in the colony.

As a child, Miguel enjoyed playing with the Native American children whose families worked on the hacienda. Many looked down upon the Native Americans, whose languages and customs were different and seemed strange. But Miguel was interested in the Native Americans and got along with them. He did not understand why these people could not own land. Hadn't they lived in the country before everyone else? And he saw that although they worked very hard, they remained very poor.

When Miguel was eight years old, his mother died giving birth to his brother. Her death was a terrible blow to Miguel. But it caused him to draw closer to his father. It was Miguel's father who taught him to read and write.

At the age of twelve, Miguel, along with his older brother, was sent away to school to study for the priesthood. They attended schools in several areas. And wherever they went, Miguel was a brilliant student. He had a passion to learn traditional subjects such as math, science, and theology—the study of religion. He also learned Native American languages such as Otomi, Tar-

This Diego Rivera mural presents the civilization of Native Americans who lived in Mexico before the Spaniards.

ascan, and Nahuatl. The more Miguel understood the Native Americans, the more he felt that what the Spaniards had done to them and others in New Spain was wrong: They had taken control of the land and the best jobs.

Miguel took exams for the priesthood at the University of Mexico. He earned a degree in theology. Then in 1779, at the age of twenty-six, he was ordained—officially declared a priest.

PRIESTHOOD · Once he became a priest, the brilliant student also became a gifted professor. In 1780, Father Hidalgo returned to one of the schools where he had studied, San Nicolás Obispo, which was run by the Catholic Church. He taught grammar, theology, and Latin. In 1784 he won twelve silver medals for writing the best essays—one in Spanish and the other in Latin—on studying religion. Success in writing and teaching led to Father Hidalgo's appointment as rector, or head of the school, in 1790.

Both good and bad things came from Hidalgo's success at San Nicolás Obispo. He established a friendship with the priest Manuel Abad y Quiepo, who would later become the bishop—an important supervisor of priests—of Michoacán. He also received a salary of five hundred gold coins, or ducats, that allowed him to buy three haciendas.

But the Catholic Church officials connected with the school did not agree with some of Hidalgo's opinions and ways of doing things. He added new, nontraditional subjects to the school, and these changes angered the officials. In 1792 they forced Father Hidalgo to leave.

Hidalgo went to a small village called San Felipe in 1793. While many priests might have chosen a quiet life in this small town, he did the opposite. He turned his house into a gathering place for the people of the region.

Father Hidalgo in his study. The paper under his hand shows the year—1810—that he began the revolt against Spain.

Not only did writers, thinkers, and musicians visit Hidalgo's house each night, but Native Americans and women—who also had few rights at that time—were welcome. People talked and exchanged ideas. One of the ideas that Hidalgo talked about was that monarchy—rule by a king and queen such as Mexico had under Spain—should be replaced by democracy, rule by the people.

Left: Hidalgo invited common people, such as this mestizo family, to his house.

Facing page: In this painting by the Spanish artist Francisco de Goya, the king of Spain, Ferdinand VII, is mounted on his horse.

Inquisition members question a priest. If they don't like his answers, they are prepared to hang him by his hands.

But just as they had done at San Nicolás Obispo, Father Hidalgo's views and methods upset Church officials, particularly those who belonged to the Inquisition. The Inquisition was an organization set up by the Catholic Church for a special purpose. That purpose was to look into activities the Church thought would harm the Church and its authority. The Inquisition did not like Father Hidalgo's talk of democracy. It felt this went against the Spanish government, which was closely tied to the Church. The Inquisition accused Hidalgo of harming the Church. It investigated him for several years but eventually dropped the charges.

In 1803, Father Hidalgo was transferred to the village of Dolores. Dolores was larger and wealthier than San Felipe. It offered Hidalgo the opportunity to expand his work with people. Hidalgo decided that one way to help people was to have them develop businesses. One business Hidalgo helped develop was silk making. He planted over one hundred mulberry trees. The leaves of these trees provide food for worms used to make silk. Hidalgo employed Native Americans to tend the trees, grow the worms, and make silk.

But the silk-making business violated a law of the Spanish government. The government wanted the colony to purchase silk only from Spain. It did not allow growing mulberry trees or raising silkworms ouside of Spain. The government also did not permit Native Americans to work at jobs like silk making.

This angered Hidalgo. He saw it as another attempt to keep the people of New Spain—especially the Native Americans—poor and dependent on Spain. He began to think it would be better to break away from the mother country.

The time appeared right for a change. In 1808, Napoleon, the ruler of France, invaded Spain. He forced the king and queen to give up the throne. The Spanish people rose up in revolt against the French, and the country was in turmoil. Hidalgo and many others thought that with Spain distracted by its own problems, Mexico had a chance to win a fight to overthrow the government—a revolution.

With a handful of others, Hidalgo began planning a revolutionary army. His associates were Ignacio Allende, Juan Aldama, Miguel Domínguez, and Domínguez's wife, María Josefa.

But news of the planning reached the Spanish authorities. When María Josefa found this out, she knew she had to tell Hidalgo. The Spaniards would arrest and perhaps even kill anyone they thought was against them. She sent a warning with Aldama, who rode through the night to Hidalgo's house. Early Sunday morning, on September 16, 1810, Aldama reached the priest and told him the news.

Hidalgo would not back down. He wanted to start the revolution immediately. That morning he ordered the ringing of his church bell to gather people together. From Dolores and the nearby haciendas people came. When they entered the church, they saw Father Hidalgo standing before them. He announced:

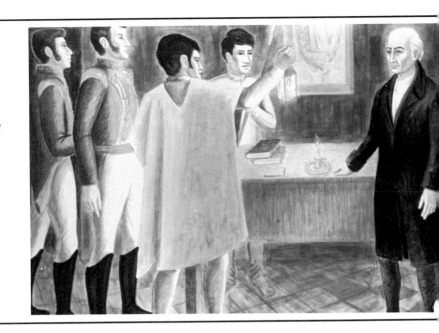

Hidalgo receives word that the Spaniards know about his plan to revolt.

Will you be free? Will you make an effort to recover from the hated Spaniards lands stolen from our forefathers long ago? Today we must act!

With those words, the priest marched down the aisle of the church with his followers behind him. Everyone shouted: "Death to the *gachupines* [Spaniards]! Down with bad government! Long live the Virgin of Guadalupe!" These words were the Cry (or, in Spanish, the *Grito*) of Dolores, the call for the Mexican War of Independence to begin.

THE VIRGIN
OF GUADALUPE

The cry "Long live the Virgin of Guadalupe!" refers to the Virgin Mary, who Christians believe is the mother of Jesus Christ. In Mexico, a famous legend surrounds this figure.

According to the legend, a poor Native American named Juan Diego was traveling over a hill called Tepeyac in Mexico City on December 9, 1531. Suddenly a shining image appeared before Diego's eyes. The image was the Virgin Mary. She told Diego that a place of worship should be built where she appeared. She directed Diego to tell the bishop of her wish. Then she disappeared.

The Virgin appearing to Juan Diego.

Diego did as he was told, but the bishop did not believe him. Three days later, the image appeared again and called herself Mary of Guadalupe.

The story of these appearances spread, and many Mexicans believed them. The Virgin of Guadalupe went on to become the national saint of Mexico and a figure of great importance to Mexicans. Statues and pictures of the Virgin are everywhere in Mexico. Every September 12, Catholics in Mexico and in the southwestern United States commemorate the Virgin's legendary appearance with a religious feast.

REVOLUTION · A crowd of Native Americans, mestizos, and Creoles gathered behind Father Hidalgo as he left the church. A few had guns, but most carried large knives called machetes, sharpened sticks, bows and arrows, or clubs. As it marched, the crowd grew. Soon there were over 50,000 people on the move from Dolores. This became Hidalgo's revolutionary army.

Hidalgo leads his army—with its symbol,
the Virgin of Guadalupe—on to
revolution in this mural by Juan O'Gorman.

Hidalgo was the captain general—the commander in chief—of the forces. Second-in-command was Ignacio Allende. The first thing Hidalgo did for his army was give it a symbol. He made a drawing of the Virgin of Guadalupe and decreed it would be the army's sign. The army began taking nearby villages and towns and proclaiming them free from Spain.

The army then headed for the city of Guanajuato. For three hundred years this city had supplied Spain with gold and silver mined in Mexico. It was a rich and important place. On reaching the city, Hidalgo discovered that his old friend Juan Antonio Riaño was defending it. Hoping to avoid violence, the priest asked for the city's surrender, promising to treat all Spaniards fairly. But he added: "If, however, those Spaniards do not decide to become our prisoners, I shall use every force to destroy them."

Riaño refused to surrender. He led his forces into a fort used to store grain, the Alhóndiga de Granaditas. Hidalgo ordered his army to attack, and Riaño was killed. The fort fell to Hidalgo's army. Guanajuato had been captured.

But Hidalgo soon lost control of his forces. They became an unruly mob and began attacking, robbing, and murdering all Spaniards. Hidalgo and Allende had to struggle to restore order. They succeeded, but word of the destruction of Guanajuato frightened the Spaniards.

The city of Guanajuato, surrounded by mountains.

When Hidalgo's army moved on to the city of Valladolid on October 17, they found that the Spanish forces there had already retreated.

In Valladolid, Hidalgo also found that officials of the Catholic Church had left him a message. His old friend Manuel Abad y Quiepo, now the bishop of Michoacán, had excommunicated him. In the Catholic Church, to be excommunicated means that the person is expelled from the religion and after death cannot enter heaven.

In Mexican artist Ramirez Joaquin's painting, Hidalgo raises his army's flag in victory at Monte de la Cruces.

Father Hidalgo took the excommunication seriously. He went into a cathedral to pray and think. But later he came out and stated that he rejected the excommunication. He laid out plans for creating the government of a new nation free from Spain. He also appealed for unity among his followers, saying:

> *If we do not fight among ourselves, the war will [end]. Let us establish a congress composed of representatives of all the cities, towns, and villages of this country. Our lawmakers will rule us with the tenderness of parents. They will treat us like brothers; they will [end] poverty.*

With new determination Hidalgo led the army to Mexico City. Mexico City was the colony's capital and most important city. If Hidalgo's army could capture it, victory could be within reach. On October 30, Hidalgo's army met Spain's forces on a mountainside outside Mexico City called Monte de las Cruces. Hidalgo's army won the fierce battle that followed. The road to the capital was opened.

Allende and others urged marching to Mexico City immediately. That way the Spaniards would not have had a chance to prepare for a fight. Hidalgo refused. Even today, no one knows why. Perhaps he felt that he did not have enough weapons or that his army was too undisciplined to take Mexico City. Whatever the reason, Hidalgo ordered his army to retreat.

THE BEGINNING OF THE END · This decision turned out to have been a grave mistake. While retreating, Hidalgo's army clashed with another Spanish force. This time, Hidalgo's army lost. They retreated further to Valladolid and then to the city of Guadalajara.

In Guadalajara, Hidalgo proclaimed freedom for all black slaves. He was the first person in the Americas to do so. He also said that lands taken by the Spaniards should be given back to the Native Americans.

Despite the bold new laws he made, Hidalgo and his army were on the run. Spanish forces had followed Hidalgo to Guadalajara. On a series of hills near the Calderón River, the two armies met for the last time. Hidalgo now had 90,000 soldiers, and the Spaniards had only 10,000. But the Spanish soldiers were better trained. On January 17, 1811, Hidalgo's revolutionary army was almost completely destroyed.

Most of the soldiers in his army scattered. The priest went to a nearby hacienda to meet with Allende. But there Allende informed him that he no longer considered Hidalgo in charge. Allende took what remained of the army and headed north.

Hidalgo then received a message from the Spanish government. It offered him a pardon for his role in the rebellion. But Hidalgo felt that to accept the pardon would mean admitting he was wrong to fight for his cause. Even though his role in the revolt was finished, Hidalgo replied:

We will not lay aside our arms until we have taken the jewel of liberty. . . . Pardon is for criminals, not defenders of their country.

But the revolution was doomed. A young officer in what was now Allende's army, Ignacio Elizondo, decided to turn over what remained of the force to the Spaniards. He was angry with Allende for not promoting him. He knew that Allende was moving north and that Father Hidalgo would follow. He also knew that they would probably stop at a well in a place called Baján so their horses could drink.

Elizondo and other soldiers set a trap at Baján. As the revolution's leaders rode up to the well, Elizondo's men captured them. When Allende arrived, he saw what was happening and reached for his gun, shouting at Elizondo: "Traitor!" But Elizondo's men fired, and Allende fell wounded.

Hidalgo arriving in the trap at Bajan.

The last to arrive was Hidalgo. When he was ordered to give up, he resisted. But he saw he was outnumbered. Slowly, he raised his hands in surrender.

The prisoners were taken by Elizondo's men to the Spanish authorities and were thrown in jail. A Spanish court tried them for treason—betraying the Spanish government. All were found guilty. All died before firing squads.

But the War of Independence did not die with Hidalgo or his followers. Another priest, José María Morelos, took up the fight against Spanish rule. He built an army and managed to gain control of most of southern Mexico. But in 1815 he was captured and shot. Two Mexicans, Vincente Guerrero and Guadalupe Victoria, continued the struggle.

Iturbide's army enters Mexico City.

Meanwhile, Spain's government began to raise taxes on New Spain and rule the colony more strictly. This frightened the Spaniards in Mexico. They thought they might begin to lose their privileges. Agustín Iturbide, a Spanish army officer who had fought against Hidalgo, joined forces with Guerrero. They worked out a compromise called the "Plan of Iguala" in which Spaniards would share their privileges with Mexicans in an independent Mexico.

On September 27, 1821, Iturbide's army marched into Mexico City and declared an end to Spanish rule. Now Mexico was free.

Mexican President Carlos Salinas de Gortari and his wife celebrating independence on September 15.

Today Miguel Hidalgo y Costilla is considered the "Father of Mexican Independence." The town of Dolores was renamed in his honor and is now called Dolores Hidalgo.

Every September 15 at midnight, the president of Mexico and mayors in every city of the country ring bells. This is to remind Mexicans of that Sunday morning in 1810 when Father Hidalgo rang his church bell to summon people to follow him on the road to freedom.

IMPORTANT EVENTS IN
THE LIFE OF
MIGUEL HIDALGO Y COSTILLA

1753   Miguel Hidalgo y Costilla is born on May 8 in Pénjamo, Mexico.

1765   Miguel leaves home to begin studying for the priesthood.

1779   Miguel is ordained and becomes Father Hidalgo.

1780–   Father Hidalgo teaches at San Nicolás Obispo and be-
1792   comes its rector. His ideas and methods anger Catholic Church officials connected with the school, and
he is forced to leave.

1803   Father Hidalgo is appointed priest of Dolores and
works to help Native Americans.

1810   On September 16, Hidalgo begins the Mexican War of
Independence with the *Grito de Dolores* (the Cry of
Dolores). On October 30 his army opens the road to
Mexico City, but he orders a retreat.

1811   On January 17, Hidalgo's army is defeated at Guadalajara. Ignacio Allende takes control, but Ignacio Elizondo turns over the revolution's leaders to the Spanish. On July 30, Miguel Hidalgo y Costilla dies before
a firing squad for treason.

1821   On September 27, Mexico becomes free from Spain.

FIND OUT MORE
ABOUT MIGUEL
HIDALGO Y COSTILLA

Father Hidalgo: A Mini-Play. Stockton, Calif.: Stevens & Shea, 1978.

Miguel Hidalgo y Costilla. Milwaukee, Wis.: Raintree, 1988.

ABOUT MEXICAN HISTORY

The Fall of Mexico City by George Ochoa. Westwood, N.J.: Silver Burdett, 1989.

The Mexican Revolution by David Killingray. San Diego, Calif.: Greenhaven, 1980.

ABOUT MEXICO

Count Your Way Through Mexico by Jim Haskins. Minneapolis, Minn.: Carolrhoda, 1989.

Mexico by Ian James. New York: Franklin Watts, 1990.

INDEX

Page numbers in *italics* refer to illustrations.